Intentionally blank

Other books by the Author

Self Help – How to get started.

Two months in America.

How to write and publish your own book for free, in 2015

What would you like to do when you grow up and leave school?

What is your Plan B?

A journey of 1,000 miles

Slick Moaner Novels

Adventures into Danger #1

Adventures above the clouds #2

Adventures of this world and others #3

Contact the author @
SimonAmazingClarke@gmail.com

DISCLAIMER AND TERMS OF USE AGREEMENT

The Author, Editor and Publisher of this book, and the accompanying materials, have used their best efforts in preparing this book. The author and publisher make no representation or warranties with respect to the accuracy, applicability, fitness, or completeness of the contents of this book. The information contained in this book is strictly for educational purposes.

Therefore, if you wish to apply ideas contained in this book, you are taking full responsibility for your actions.

The Author, Editor and Publisher disclaim any warranties (express or implied), merchantability, or fitness for any particular purpose. The author and publisher shall in no event be held liable to any party for any direct, indirect, punitive, special, incidental or other consequential damages arising directly or indirectly from any use of this material, which is provided "as is", and without warranties.

As always, the advice of a competent legal, tax, accounting, medical or other appropriate professional should be sought.

The Author, Editor and Publisher do not warrant the performance, effectiveness or applicability of any sites listed or linked to in this book.

All links are for information purposes only and are not warranted for content, accuracy or any other implied or explicit purpose.

This book is © copyrighted by Simon 'Amazing' Clarke. No part of this may be copied, or changed in any format, sold, or used in any way other than what is outlined within this book under any circumstances.

This will blow your socks off

By
Simon A Clarke

Notes on the Author

I've been interested in all things that fly from my earliest days. I used to watch seagulls flying in the air currents near where I grew up. Having joined the RAF as an aircraft engineer, I grew a greater appreciation for all things that fly.

About twenty years ago I got a copy of Timothy Good's book, 'Above Top Secret,' that really opened my eyes to the fact that UFOs, as they were called, are apparently, real and not just figments of people's imagination.

I followed this on with Nick Cook's book, 'The hunt for Zero Point.' I really got to see that there was so much more that I didn't understand, and so many more facts out there, that I had never thought of. That is where I began my initial research for this book. What most impressed me, and continues to impress me, is the fact that almost daily I uncover new information or discover new places that are worth my while investigating.

Notes on this book

Have you ever looked into getting a book published? It's not easy. In fact it's ten times harder than writing the book in the first place. I would like to apologise now for any mistakes that you find in this book. I have done my best to make it as interesting as I can for everyone who reads it, but unfortunately it will not be to everyone's liking. If you do come across any mistakes please feel free to email me and identify them. I appreciate everyone's input that helps me turn this book into the best product that I can produce. Who knows, if I sell enough of them I could afford to get it professionally edited or even picked up by a big publishing company.

Introduction

What we are told today about the history of mankind is wrong! I know that it is a very bold statement, but as you read in this book, the facts will slowly be revealed to you.

The first questions that most people ask when they hear me say that are, how it is wrong, why is it wrong and whose fault is it?

Firstly it isn't anyone's fault. It is not governments or any secret society's fault. It's just the way that we have evolved intellectually over the last 1,000 years.

What seems to have happened time and time again is that we have had knowledge and then lost it. Let me give you an example. In the middle ages, around the 1500's, the world was considered to be flat, and was the centre of the universe. Anyone who disagreed with the Church, or the nation's top scientists of the day, were either considered lunatics or stood a good chance of losing their heads. But, if we go back a thousand years to the ancient Egyptians, they knew that we were on a round planet and that we orbit the sun. They also knew the position of the other planets in our solar system including the outer rocky planets. I'll come back to that later on.

Let me give you another example of knowledge gained then lost. In the early 1980's when I was doing my aircraft engineering training I was introduced to Brahms's Press principle for Hydraulics. In the 1800's, Brahms discovered the principles of hydraulics that we use today in all modern mechanical machinery. But, here again, what we are told is wrong. The Romans were doing all sorts of things with water 2,000 years ago, including making it run up hill and pressurising it to work in fountains. Therefore they were using the water-press principle, before Brahms.

So to the question, why are we being given the wrong information?

From what I have been able to work out, the situation is twofold. Firstly if something has been invented then forgotten about, and someone reinvents it, then it is usually the latter person that we know about, as is the case with hydraulics. The other thing that happens is that someone invents something but doesn't do anything with it. Another person separately invents it but then does something with it. Hmm, that sounds a little confusing. Let me give you an example. There are three or four people who claim the right to be called the first to fly a powered aircraft. Santos Dumont invented a flying machine that first flew a couple of years before the Wright brothers. After his flight he parked the aircraft in a hanger and left it. The Wright brothers on the other hand knew that flying their aircraft was to be a world changing event, so they got the press involved at the earliest opportunity. Also, once they started flying, they kept on redesigning their aircraft and looked at selling them to the military as spotter aircraft. That is the main reason why they are so well known. It is a little known fact that the Short Brothers of Northern Ireland built a Wright Flyer for the Wright brothers in 1909 to use when they came over to Europe to sell to the European armies. This made the Short brother the first aircraft contract builders in the world.

Now we come into another problem. Let's say that someone comes up with solid evidence to say that someone else flew two months before the Wright brothers did. It will take a lot of convincing to have the public change their view on the history as they know it.

This is the case for Chuck Yeager, the second man to fly faster than the speed of sound. Now if you are an aviation enthusiast, you will be shaking your head right now thinking that I am wrong. Well, the evidence is that George Walsh was the first person to fly faster than the speed of sound. Actually he did it in a pre-production model of the F-86 Sabre a couple of days before Chucks 'Famous' flight.

In the case of the Wright brothers, I do know that Santos Dumont is credited with the first powered flight of a heavier than air aircraft and that the Wright brothers were credited with the first powered controlled flight. The big difference being that the Wrights could control their aircraft whereas Santos had to rely purely on stability.

I did read recently (early 2015) that there is a new challenger to the Wright's flight. I haven't read up on that yet, but if it is found to be true, the hard part will be changing people's perspective.

That is also the problem that I am going to have with this book. I am going to give you facts. Some of these new facts are going to be hard to follow so please remember, if you disagree with what I have written, you will have to come up with facts that prove that I am wrong. Just because you think I am wrong, doesn't make you right.

Chapter - 1

Firstly and most importantly, this book is my interpretation of what I have found and seen. The point is this, we don't know what the truth is, about our ancestors. They might have had greater knowledge than we give them credit for, or we could have been helped by extra-terrestrials. All we have are clues. While I've done my best to gain as much insight as I can from the clues I've come across, this is from an inquisitive engineer's viewpoint and not from an archaeological one.

It has always been my aim with anything that I have found out of the ordinary to ask and answer, as well as possible, the following questions. Could man, at that time, have made this possible? Could technology from somewhere else in the world have been used here? Or, is the technology used, way beyond human capability.

To answer the last two questions I used the following parameters. Technology from elsewhere in the world would be similar to the Europeans bringing the horse and cart to North America in the 1500's. That sort of technology would be alien to the North American Indians.

To answer the last question, is it beyond human capability, I use the last fifty years as the bench mark. When I come across something that was not possible fifty years ago and maybe we could just about manage it in the early twenty first century, then I feel that we may have to look to the stars to find the answers as to how it was achieved. As an example of this, I look to the 1,200 ton stones of Baalbek in Lebanon. These immense stones are 14 ft. square and 70 ft. long. The average density of stone is 2.5 tonnes per cubic metre. The really significant part of this story is that they were carved and moved before the time of the Romans. We would struggle to move stones of this size today, so how did people move them thousands of years ago?

Let's look at something else a little different. If we were to get someone from Europe and North America, and test them against natives from South America, Australia, India and China and present them all with logic problems that didn't require knowledge of mathematics or engineering, we would find that the results would be similar. There is no difference between the cognitive power of the human brain anywhere in the world, and we are as intelligent now as we were 10,000 years ago. Actually, this level of intelligence goes back a lot further, as you will find out shortly.

So let's get started with our journey, where do we humans come from? Who are our ancestors? When did we humans become intelligent?

I am fascinated by history. Now, don't worry, I'm not talking about the Kings and Queens of England or all of the American Presidents. I'm talking about our ancient history, before the Romans, Greeks and Egyptians. I'll start off with the questions above and explain where we came from. Then I will move on to how we developed. This is where we start to ask the really deep questions like, were we helped by Aliens?

Aliens, now there is a word that evokes all kinds of thoughts and emotions within people from the, 'but they don't exist?' to the, 'they have done everything for us?' Just so that you know where I stand on this, for the purposes of this book, I know of at least two species that live in America and no, as far as I am aware, I have not been abducted, yet.

I'm obviously talking about the little green men and the 'Greys', and any other Aliens that have influenced us, and our planet, over the millennia's.

Did I lose you there? I'm sorry. Let me start off nice and slowly, and easy you in to this.

Most of what I present in this book is information that I have collected from other people's works. The internet is an amazing tool in the early 21st century. There are articles to read on every topic that you could think of. Not only that, but you can also watch videos of people in the actual place that you want to visit. It's nearly the same as being there yourself, almost, but not quite.

I present in this book the information that I agree with, I'm not saying that this are the only truths out there, but there are some things that even I struggle to comprehend. There are several groups and individuals that have presentations on the, 'Hollow Earth Theory,' I struggle getting my head around that one, so I don't cover it in this book.

Once I have covered the part about where we come from I'll get into the best part of this book, the last 10,000 years. Prior to that time we hadn't built much, our technology was advanced but still relatively primitive. Flint axes and knives seem low tech to us today but to the peoples of the time they were life changing. You didn't have to rely on your teeth, fingers and nails to do everything. The Clovis people, in North America, knew this so well. That's why when they brought their technology from southern France and Spain they thrived in the North American Continent. Yes, around 13,000 BC Europeans reached America. That's 14,500 years before Christopher Columbus.

Although I am not an archaeologist I have been an engineer for over 30 years and I can see how things are done. Archaeologists look for the small pieces of information to see how people lived. It is my intention, with this book, to see what they did and how they did it.

As an example of this, I can understand ancient man creating the ring of stones on the island of Lewis in Scotland, but I can't see how Stonehenge was created.

I can visualise in my mind people coming together to move stones, digging holes and placing them in it. It's the complexities of Stonehenge that I consider above the human ingenuity of the time. One question of any stone circle is why? Why did some people spend that amount of time and effort moving the stones into the circles, what do the circle mean? Are they really early forms of calendars? Or are they meant to be something else entirely?

Also, if you would like to learn more about the truths that I reveal in this book I am available for talks of all sorts of shapes and sizes. Do book early though, as my calendar fills up quickly.

Chapter - 2

Here is a fact I love to share. In his book, 'a short history of nearly everything' by Bill Bryson, he relates a story of when he was taken to a dried up lake bed somewhere in Africa and scattered around were flint fragments. There were actually so many flint fragments, that this whole area was several feet thick with them. He was told that for over a million years this is where flints were shaped into tools like hand axes and knives. The best part thought, was that the people who did this work were not humans!

There are many reasons why a lot of the information that is out there is not, 'main stream' knowledge That's because it doesn't fit in with the current paradigm.

Let me give you an example of the 'current' knowledge being wrong.

A Frenchman was interested in learning what the Egyptian pictures that were carved all over Egypt meant. When he asked his archaeology professor about this he was told. "They are not important. They are only pictures".

This happened in the 1800's, and it is fortunate for us today, that this man, and an Englishman, did persist with their desire to decipher what they thought was a pictorial language. One of the things that was found in Egypt was a rock called the Rosetta stone. After the Greeks had fought the Egyptians and won, they had stones carved in three different languages. When these two men were deciphering these scripts they could easily read the first one which was quite well known to scholars at the time as ancient Greek, the second language was in what we would call, modern Egyptian. As this was translated, it was realised that it was the same message as was written in Greek. Basically the Greeks were telling the Egyptians that they had conquered their lands and that they were now under Greek command.

Both of the men looked at the third set of writing and assumed that the hieroglyphic pictograms would contain the same message. Both men went through ridicule and great personal loss to prove their point, and fortunately for them, they both came up with the same answers independently so providing, indisputable proof, that the pictures were indeed a language to be read, and not just pretty pictures.

Chapter - 3

Going back to the Bill Bryson book, I can't remember if Bill ever reveals who had made these flint tools, but I suspect it was Neolithic man or one of the other early humanoid peoples. There were several 'species' (for want of a better word) that were bipedal intelligent apes that developed from our ancestral tree, but all have died out and therefore, they were not one of our direct ancestors.

Quite often the simplest way to create something is the easiest, quickest and cheapest way of doing it. As an example, would you create a block of stone that weights 100 lbs or one that weights 100 tons? You need a lot of 100 lbs blocks to build something, but they are a lot easier to move. 100 ton stones are a lot quicker to make, (there is a lot less flat surfaces to carve) but they are incredibly difficult to move. If I was tasked with this job I would have several rocks created of different weights and see which was the quickest to create and get to where I wanted it. It might be found that a 1 ton or 5 ton stone would be the more optimised. It's about getting the greatest volume of rock moved to the building site in the shortest amount of time. To give you a practical example look at the size of stone that was used to build English churches or look at the biggest stones that the Romans used.

Just to give you an idea of size, a 12 inch cube of Stone, i.e. 1 cubic foot, weighs 140 lbs.

There is evidence of incredibly complex carved rock, but there has been nothing found to show how these incredible feats have been achieved and no evidence of the people who made them.

In most of these cases, the sites have been dated by the evidence found which I think is when these were inhabited far later, after they were initially built and later abandoned.

I must disagree with some of the archaeologists here. If the only pottery you found is dated to 200 years ago, it doesn't always mean that this place was built then by these people. It just means that someone lived there 200 years ago.

Think of an abandoned castle in Scotland, the whole place was stripped out 500 years ago but some people lived in the ruins 200 years ago, if this was the only evidence you had, what date would you put on it? That is, based on the evidence in front of you.

I know archaeology isn't that simple, they do go into great depths to find out all of the information that they can, but as scientists, it is their duty to only deliver details on the facts that they have, and any other thoughts and ideas that can't be proven have to be left out of their reports. They also have to stick to the current paradigm. Archaeologists have time frames for everything. If the evidence they have falls out of this time line then if they were to report that date, they would face ridicule from their colleagues. It's a lot safer to push the boundaries of the current time line.

I have a bit of a quandary now. How do I lead you in to what I have come across? Do I just throw you in at the deep end, or guide you in slowly?

Ok, I'm going to throw you in fully clothed into the deep end, and I hope you can swim.

Have you ever heard of Ley lines? In the 1920's Alfred Watkins walked all over the UK and he noticed that Churches and ancient monuments seemed to run in lines. Thinking that a straight line was the quickest route from A to B, he thought that he would follow these straight lines and see if his theory was correct. What Watkins found were swamps and impassable rivers. Confused, he started marking these on a map and published a book about his findings.

It appears that all over the UK there are natural power lines that run through the earth. The interesting fact is that they are not just limited to the UK, they extend all over the world.

If you plot these lines on a map of the world you see that they cross each other at regular intervals. Where they cross is most fascinating.

Have a look on the internet for the 'World Grid Points', I think it's awesome.

One of these intersection places is near the island of Bermuda, just off the coast of Florida. Another one is sat on top of Easter Island. Another is where Cairo is and the great pyramids.

Have a look for yourself at where some of the other lines meet. Some places you will recognise, some you won't, and we will come on to those in later chapters.

If you are reading this book I will assume that you know of the Bermuda Triangle. If not, it is a place where a lot of ships and aeroplanes have gone missing over the years.

Easter Island, again for those who don't know, is an island in the pacific, miles away from anywhere. I think the closest land is Chile, and that is over 900 miles away. The really odd thing about Easter Island is the enormous statues that were built there. The time and effort taken to produce these, on what is a small island, is incredible. Also, it shows ingenuity that is not found anywhere else in the Pacific!

A lot of people have seen the impressive pictures of the heads on Easter Island, but what most people don't realise is that they are not just heads, they are actually statues that are over 30 to 40 feet tall, plus a section that would have been buried to hold the statue upright.

So let me ask you a question. How long would it take the ground to increase in height to cover a 15 feet statue?

As a rough rule of thumb for the UK, and I don't know if it is the same the world over, but the ground increases in height at the rate of 1 inch per one hundred years.

15 times 12 times 100 equals 18,000 years. So were these statues made and erected 18,000 years ago? If so by whom and with what technology?

Chapter - 4

Let's look at some other totally amazing facts that will blow your socks off.

When the tombs of some of the early mummies were opened in Egypt between the 1920's and 1950's, they discovered items that, I think, have mainly been glossed over.

We know about the elaborate chambers, and all of the amazing artefacts that the great pharaohs were buried with, but there are a couple of things, that you might or might not have heard about.

So let's get on to what was found that is so outstanding. It was Cocoa Beans and Cocaine.

Reading that you might be thinking, what is so exciting or extraordinary about those? Your right in thinking that they are ordinary every day types of things today (except that cocaine is illegal in our society).

Before I reveal the big bombshell, let's just remind ourselves when these tombs were sealed, we are talking about 4,500 years ago.

Just in case you are unsure about world trade and commodities etc. Cocoa Beans originated in South America. None were grown anywhere else until the plants and seeds were shipped from the new world to the old world (Europe).

Let me just remind you of something else, Christopher Columbus discovered America in 1492 AD. Hmm, we have a problem here. The Cocoa beans in these tombs had already been sat in the tombs for over 4,000 years by then. Now does that mean that someone has discovered time travel, no, we will look into who was visiting South America later on in the book.

Before we look into how these beans got there let's look at Cocaine. Ok, so I had to look this up. I wasn't sure how cocaine was made, but I had a feeling that it involves using several chemicals. It certainly does, it's actually quite an involved process. I also noticed on the website that I looked on, that a lot of it is made in Bolivia. That is an interesting clue, you will see why, again, later on in the book.

So the big question here is, how did products from these two plants get from one side of the Atlantic to the other?

Basically there are two routes, the first is across the Atlantic, the second is the long way across the world via the middle east, China and across the Bearing Straits then follow down into what is now Canada down into continental America, across Central America and there you are.

Which of these do you think is possible and more probable 4,500 years ago? The simple answer is neither. But the fact remains the evidence is there.

How could the Egyptians possibly know of other continents, especially across the vast Atlantic Ocean? What really surprises me, are the really ancient maps. There are several, but the one that really interests me is the Piri Reis map. Captain Piri Reis was a 16th century Turkish Captain. He wrote on his map that he had copied several ancient source maps to produce his map. That might not sound to spectacular in itself but his 1513 map shows many unusual coast lines, many of these, by this time, undiscovered by sailors.

The map shows Antarctica. This was not discovered until 1773 and the shape of the land mass wasn't actually known until the 1950's when it was mapped by radar. All of this is interesting but the Piri Reis map shows the shape of the Antarctic continental land mass.

Also the map clearly shows both the coast of Africa and that of South America. It shows the west coast of Africa and the east coast of South America. One of the strange things about this map is that it shows South America connecting to Antarctica, which it obviously doesn't.

But it did, 12,000 years ago during the last ice age! This map, and several others, show the world how it looked back then. When the sea level was over 400ft (120m) lower.

This I feel is enormous evidence that there were vastly more technically advanced 'humans' living here at the time. I put the words humans in quotation marks because I don't know if they were humans like us, or Anunnaki humans, as in, 'those who from heaven to earth came.'

Just too close of this chapter I want to give you a teaser. There have been sculptures found in South America showing African types of faces, but these carvings were made thousands of years ago. How can this be possible?

Chapter - 5

So enough of our early wanderings for now, let's look at the birth of the human race.

Where do human beings really come from?

Let me take you back to a hundred million years ago. At the same time as the cold blooded dinosaurs roamed the earth there were small warm blooded animals, the ancestors of the mammals. These lived side by side with the dinosaurs. Most of them were very small, like modern day shrews or mice. If they grew any bigger they would become a potential food source for the dinosaurs, so they stayed the same size.

Even before the massive impact that wiped out the remaining dinosaurs, a lot of them were dying out. But, due to their diminutive size, the early mammals survived the hard times and went on to repopulate the entire world.

During the last 65 million years of the land domination by mammalian species, some have developed, but a lot had come and gone even before we got our hands on the planet.

Some of our ancestors took to climbing trees instead of walking along on all fours, these developed into monkeys and apes and continued to do so until, due to climatic or other changes, one ape did something different. It is due to what Lucy did, that we have developed into the people that we are today. She stood up and walked on two legs. Her species, Australopithecus, were, because of this simple act, to start the biological changes that lead to us. As more and more of her kind started to follow suit their bodies began to change.

Lucy, as the skeletal remains have been called, was the first to start making these changes. Over the following two million years there have been a number of identifiable changes that has meant that different sub species have evolved. Our hands changed from being able to grip branches to allowing us to grip tools. An opposable thumb not only allows us to touch each of our fingers with our thumb, but it allows us to be able to hold tools in different ways and gives us the dexterity that we have today.

As we were able to hold tools, we then had the ability to hunt instead of just collecting fruit. Eating meat was far more energy efficient, and with the amount that we were consuming, our brains started to grow. Not many people are aware how much energy the brain actually consumes. If you have had a day at work where you have had to do a lot of thinking, your body can feel fatigue, just like if it has been doing exercise. This is due to the amount of energy that the brain has consumed.

Also, as our brains grew, and we consumed more meat, our digestive system changed. Instead of requiring a big gut to process a vegetarian diet, it could reduce, resulting in a humanoid body that was a lot leaner, more resembling our bodies today.

All of this resulted in the final model around 250,000 years ago with us, well nearly.

Throughout the evolution of the human being, there were, at times, several humanoid species. In fact, in some area's several species existed at the same time. There have been some fossil humanoids that have been found in the same area at the same geological time zone that were quite different and obviously from different species.

There have also been several great extinctions, in some areas early humanoid evidence can be gathered up to a certain period in time and then there is nothing for a few thousand years.

In some of these extinctions, we humans, were lucky to have survived at all. It is thought that, during one such extinction, the human population dropped to as little as a few hundred individuals. It is from this common ancestor that we are all related.

The humans of 120,000 years ago, are just the same as us. They have the same brain function, the same cognitive ability, the same eyes etc. Yes, they might have looked a little different to us, but if you were to place them in a large multi-cultural office today, they wouldn't stick out more than anyone else.

These, our first true ancient ancestors, lived from 250,000 years ago until around 50,000 years ago in relative peace and harmony in Africa. Then it all changed.

What I really hadn't read up on before, when I released this book for the first time, was that 250,000 years ago in human evolution, is a very significant date. Prior to this date we were bipedal apes. Around this time we changed. It has often been said that there is a missing link. That is partially true. But with the amount of physical changes that occurred, and with the changes to our DNA, there is not enough time between these bipedal apes and us, for all of these changes to occur. In fact these changes didn't happen slowly over time. They changed in a blink of an eye. For this there is only one explanation. It is what we can read in the Sumerian tablets. The DNA from these bipedal apes was taken and modified and we were produced. We are too different from our ape ancestors.

70,000 years ago an ice age started What started this, we will cover in a later chapter but for now we will stick with what our ancestors did to cope with the changing conditions.

Something that I hadn't been aware of was that during an ice age, water becomes scarce. Also, as we know, sea levels drop. There is a cave in Southern Africa that faces the sea today, the same as it did 120,000 years ago when it was first used. Its use dropped around 50,000 years ago. This was probably due to the sea level drop causing the sea shore to be 40 km away!

The route that our ancestors took can now be followed by the use of DNA and its markers, the slight genetic changes in the male part of the sequence.

There is a great documentary on YouTube that details one Doctor's quest to follow his ancestors' route across the world.

He makes a great many shocking finds along the way. The first one is that there is a tribe in Africa that all humans are closely related too, and are the ones that we are all descended from!

Here is a great fact that I came across many years ago. If you go to any Zoo in the world and check the DNA of half a dozen Chimpanzees, you will find more genetic diversity in those six individuals, than you will in the entire human race. We really are one big family.

50,000 years ago is also the time of the biggest change of human abilities and seemed to spark not only another big change in human abilities, but also set people off travelling and spreading through the world.

Only a couple of years ago, remains were found of a settlement in South America dating back 50,000 years.

This point in time also coincides with a major ice age so travel between some current continents and islands could be accomplished by just walking from place to place. For example modern day Indonesia and Australia were part of the same single continent.

It is difficult to find much, if any, evidence of the physical journey as most of the areas that these people travelled on are now hundreds of feet underwater, but the DNA evidence is still there. As people travelled, some parts of a group would stay in one place and others would carry on. This left a trail where the DNA can still be traced today.

Chapter – 6

Not long after I started putting this book together, I was fortunate enough to be offered a job nearly three hundred miles away from home. Oh how lucky I am! The first thing I did was to see what was in the area that I would like to see, and what also might be useful for this book. As it turns out, moving (at least temporarily) down south, has several advantages. Firstly there is a lot to do and see in Bournemouth, especially if you are there over a Bank holiday. Secondly Stonehenge is only an hour up the road.

Unfortunately I have to report that the assumptions about Stonehenge are completely wrong. I'll update this statement. I was watching a documentary about TV shows featuring Stonehenge since the 1950's. Two things soon became clear. Firstly Archaeologists can't agree what Stonehenge was built for, or who built it. Secondly they all focussed on the evidence that they could dig up, but no-one looked at what had been built. The construction requires immense engineering, mathematical calculations and the ability to be able to draw and measure angles.

It's not that they have any of their facts wrong, they are totally right in everything that they have found.

The problem is the technology. At Stonehenge there is a mock-up of a large, 30 ton stone, that is strapped to some flattened logs that are sat on round logs. Some people might think, 'And, what's wrong with that?' Well, the bronze age arrived in Britain at around the same time. Actually that is a coincidence worth investigating as well. The Iron Age did not start until 3,000 years ago. So if you, perhaps, have bronze tools, how are you going to cut down trees and make them fairly round? Even with Iron Age tools, it's fairly difficult to get the logs circular and of the same diameter. You would need a basic lathe of some sorts to do that fairly accurately. If the logs were different sizes, and lumpy, then trying to move a 30 ton stone becomes very difficult.

There is also the issue of the condition of the ground. It's OK having logs under a large stone and doing this as an experiment, but in the real world if you had 6 logs under a 30 ton stone, then each log is supporting 5 tons. 5 tons pressing down on a log that is resting on soil is going to compress the soil. This compression means that as you exert a force on the rock it will have the effect of trying to roll the log up the side of the indentation that it has just made.

There is also the issue of what route they took. When I first visualised this in my mind I pictured them laying the logs along roads. The problem is that we didn't have roads until the romans came 2,500 years later. The wheel didn't arrive in Britain until 2,500 years ago. So all routes were pathways used by people and horses.

I must conduct some representative experiments on this. I want to find out what will roll and what will not.

The next issue that I have is this. If you have the technology to move these types of stones then why are you still living in a 20 foot round house? There are people in Africa today living in similar type houses.

The next thing I want to mention is the architecture. When some people look at Stonehenge today, they just see a small ramshackle collection of stones.

I'll tell you what I saw. 1, There are nodules on the top of the vertical stones. How did they know to add these and how did they manage to align it all? 2, With these in place, what caused some of the stones to fall off? There must have been one almighty explosion or something. Actually it might not have been an explosion because parts are missing from the opposite side of the Henge from what I can remember. This is without thinking about the angle of the topping stones. Let me ask you a question. You are making a circle of twenty stones, what angle do you cut the end of those stones?

A circle is 360 degrees, divide that by twenty stones and you get 18 degrees, right? Wrong. You need to cut that angle in half and divide it between the two rocks. Each will have an end angle of 9 degrees. Next question, how do you mark out 9 degrees on a rock?

There was one more thing that caught my eye. It's called Stonehenge Circus, and I tell you what, to me, it looks remarkably like a runway from the air.

To sum all of that up, it's difficult to put a date on, from modern times, when Stonehenge could have been built. I don't know if technology was advanced enough by the 1500's for it to have been built then. Even today, 30 tons is a lot to move. Especially when you need the precision to be able to line up several vertical stones so that you can cap them with the horizontal ones. Any device that you build to lift them, must be able to support the weight of itself, and the stone it is lifting.

The purpose of this book is to identify certain areas of the world and certain time frames that seem to match up. This book will not give you all of the answers that you seek. Like my visit to Stonehenge, I came away with more questions than answers.

An obvious question to ask is, what is the figure 4,500 years ago based on. Is it based upon the finds, or is it from Carbon dating the rock from under the base of a vertical stone. I'd also be interested in carbon dating a piece from under one of the fallen rocks. This would give us an idea of a date when it collapsed.

Question, if you crash landed somewhere that was populated by hostile natives, would you for example, build them something that they could use for religious purposes?

From an architectural point of view, Stonehenge is incredible. To build it, you would needed to have design it first. Usually this means drawings or/and written notes. Did someone hold all of this in his head? I seriously doubt it. It would have taken quite a number of people to organise the whole build, and therefore dimensions etc. would have required communicating.

Something else that is missing from the landscape, are any similar, but smaller Henges. Usually there would be small somethings in one area that predate the bigger something nearby. I know that there are other stone circles in the UK and it would be interesting to check the circularity of these, and noting the dates they were constructed. But, as far as I am aware, there isn't a single megalithic construction with Horizontal structures on anywhere else in the UK or northern Europe of a similar time frame.

Let me roll in some more details here.

Early man could not have produced the shape standard required to produce the rollers with Bronze tools. Rollers, especially for this type of load require being equal in size to their neighbours. Also rollers will not roll on soft ground. I would say that a full width sled made of lengthwise, logs would have been a better solution. For this thought a road would have needed to have been prepared that followed gentle contours along its route. Therefore the Sarsen stoned might have actually travelled closer to 50 miles to follow a smoother route. This route would have required surveying.

Do you know how hard it is to create rollers for a sled to carry a 5 ton load? It's actually very hard. The difficulty is in producing a roller that is the same diameter through its length and then producing all of the rollers to that size. You might think that even with a wood turning Lathe it would be easy, but it's not.

You can make something that looks round but there will be variances in diameter. You can make an attachment for a lathe that will hold your cutting tool that will make perfectly round rollers.

Shipbuilders, and other wood working trades, use a tool called an Adze. This consists of a wooden shaft two to three feet long and a steel head that is curved to the same curve as the radius of the circle from the end of the handle to the head. This tool is used to shape wood, similar to an axe, but instead of the blade being vertical like an axe, it is horizontal.

If you wanted to make fence posts for your garden you could use an Adze, and make a reasonable job of it, but you would struggle to make a round roller. You would also find it extremely difficult to make a collection of them all to the same diameter.

Oh, I nearly forgot. They didn't have steel when Stonehenge was built. In fact they were barely into the bronze age! I think I mentioned that before. OK, so why am I being so pedantic about the rollers being round and the same diameter? If you have different size rollers, the larger ones will take a greater proportion of the load, therefore they will be the ones that will sink the most, and increase the drag. If the logs are not round, but a little lumpy, then these flat spots will not roll as easy, again increasing the drag. True, the high and low spots would equal themselves out a bit, but I would reckon that it would increase the pulling force by an additional 10%.

So, what pulling force is required to move something of 5 tons or 28 tons. Firstly, that is the weight of the stone and not of everything that is being moved. With the limited abilities of the time, I'd suggest that the structure required to hold the stones would be around 25% of the weight of the stones weight so that is 1.25 tons and 7 tons respectively. Whether using a sledge or rollers, there is a rolling resistance. The force required to pull something will always be less than the force required to lift it, but the percentage of friction depends upon the surfaces involved. Railway rolling stock probably has the lowest resistance as steel on steels has very little resistance which is great when a train is moving but setting off and braking all has to be carried out slowly. A tyre on Tarmac has a higher friction so that allows us to have greater acceleration and braking ability in our cars. A rock on a sled on flat ground or on rollers would produce up to 25% friction.

5 ton rock, 1.25 ton structure = 6.25 tons. 25% friction = 1.56 tons or 1,563 kg of force.

28 ton rock, 7 ton structure = 35 tons. 25% friction = 8.75 tons or 8,750 kg of force.

We still haven't finished adding weight on yet because the ropes used to pull these stones will also have a significant weight.

Modern nylon ropes are very light weight compared to the fibre ropes of the 1800's. The ones used to pull these sleds would have been heavier still. I'd even go so far as to say that the rope would weigh 10% of the total Mass.

6.25 tons. 10% rope = 0.63 tons add 25% friction = 1.72 tons or 1,718 kg of force.

35 tons. 10% rope = 3.5 tons add 25% friction = 9.63 tons or 9,625 kg of force.

So the next question is how many people would it take to move these stones? Well, firstly, if it is on flat ground, the pulling force is as shown above, but for every 1% in incline, the pulling force increases by 1%.

If you have ever had to push a car, you will know that although you need to apply a lot of force to getting it moving, that force drops off significantly as the car starts to roll. The second thing that you will notice is that although it is easier to get it moving, pushing a car for 100m/yards takes a lot of energy and we soon tire. You will also notice that once the road starts to go uphill, if there is only you pushing the car, it will get very heavy, very quickly. I know I have had several cars that have needed to be push started.

So what force can the average person pull? We can all pull a greater weight for a short period of time but if you wanted someone to pull on a rope for several hours a day I would suggest a constant pulling figure of only 20kg (44 lbs) would be a maximum figure.

Therefore our two stones would require a minimum or 85 and 481 people to move them. If you wanted to pull the rock a couple of miles per day, I'd say that they would need to at least double or triple those numbers. Obviously increasing the numbers of people means more rope and more weight.

A ten per-cent incline would require 95 and 529 people as minimums, again, doubling and tripling would be required.

Certainly for the Sarsen stones, that is a lot of people. Let's assume that you have two pulling teams equalling 1,000 people, you then need to look after and feed them. There might also be a requirement to guard these people from marauding mobs. That would probably add another 500 people to the mix. That's a lot of people to feed and house.

Something else came to light on a recent archaeological dig near Stonehenge. There are tons of stone chips, indicating that the stones were quarried then brought to the area before they were chipped away to make then square and to the length required. That means that these blocks were a lot heavier than their final weight when they were brought to the area, so you can increase my figures.

There is also the question of how the stones were shaped. There are suggestions that people used hand stones to chip away at the rough stones to shape them. I think that is highly unlikely, I don't see any way that you could accurately create a rectangular stone that well by bashing a hand held stone on it. Bronze chisels wouldn't have done it. I think that the only thing possible for creating these stones is by using steel or something stronger!

People will say yes, but where is the evidence for this. The answer is simple It's no-where to be found, just like the Stones of Baalbek, the pyramids and a host of other places around the world.

Now here is something to consider, when the stones for Stonehenge were moved, the mathematics that I have just used had not been invented! Not in the UK anyway.

Secondly, how do you convey your ideas between so many people when you haven't got a written or, apparently, a verbal language!

There are a couple of other things to consider, the archaeologist tell us that the 5 ton stones were floated down the river Avon. You are as intelligent as a man from around this time, actually you have more knowledge because you have been to school and have had mathematical and scientific training. So let me ask you this question. How would you build a boat to carry a rock that you don't know the weight of? How many trees would you need to cut down? How are you going to cut the trees into planks to build your boat with only stone tools? Or you might decide to just fasten the logs together and place the stone on what is effectively, a giant raft.

To be honest, I couldn't work it out. It depends upon the volume of the boat that you have created or the reserve volume of the various logs. There are ways that you can work all of this out without mathematics, but it would require building lever systems and testing the boats.

There is also the issue that most people don't mention, it's easy to work out how pull a sled with a 30 ton stone on it, but there is a lot of work getting the stone into that position in the first place. The cutting of the stone from the rock face, the separating of the rock from the bed rock, and how the heck do you move a stone, that size, onto a sled.

That is a lot of effort to move stones from one place to another.

I haven't even mentioned yet about the nodules on top of the Stones and how they would need to be worked out, nor have I questioned how you make a great circle like that level enough so that when you place all of your capping stones on, and have it level.

I could go on, but I'll stop there. I think that I have already provided enough evidence to prove that late Stone Age man could not possibly have built Stonehenge. Even the Romans 2,000 years later limited themselves to about 5 tons, but they had the benefit of wheels, better ropes and pulley blocks.

So here is the tricky question, who did build Stonehenge, or more importantly, who organised and moved these enormous stones.

Firstly to these people, lifting close to 40 tons would not have been an issue. It would be like going back in time with a low loader and a large crane, then it would be relatively easy to move these stones.

Then we ask the question, Why? This is an enormous amount of effort to create something. While the build is not on the same scale as the pyramids, it is certainly more technologically advanced.

I'm not able to answer the burning question as to who built them. What I will say is that they were not from what we now know as Europe.

Were they from this world? We'll come back onto that one later in the book.

Chapter - 7

In 1978 the first test tube baby was born and since then there have been thousands of couples helped. What most people don't know is the process.

Sometimes a woman can't conceive because her body doesn't create the right environment for the developing foetus. To help the baby grow you can take the egg and the sperm from the parents and embed the egg inside a host body. This is where foster wombs come in. The child is still yours genetically (mostly) but another person is used.

The reason why I am telling you this, is that there was something interesting found in the 1930's.

The skull has been christened 'The Star Child' and it is absolutely amazing.

Not only is it strangely shaped and sized, it's the composition of the skull that is really the most interesting. Where samples of the skull have been taken it is noticed that the skull is dramatically thinner, but because of the composition it was just as strong, if not stronger, than conventional human skulls. It's like comparing aluminium to carbon fibre composite, the modern composite is stronger than the metal.

Also, there are fibres within the bones that the blade cutting the skull didn't cut. They just skidded over! This was a high speed steel blade.

The most interesting part was when they tested the DNA of the skull. A lot of the (I don't know the correct terminology) DNA strands were human and identified. There were however, over 200 DNA strands that were not of human origin!!!!!!

So there is an obvious question. Actually two. 1 What are the other DNA's? 2 How did this happened?

The happening part is really interesting. The Egg and Sperm, both none human, were fertilised then implanted in a human, then the remainder of the pregnancy and birth would have been by a human!

Let's use the word Alien, meaning none human. So an Alien fertilised egg was implanted into a human woman who had a full pregnancy and gave birth, when did I say, 1930?

Actually, 1930 is when this scull was found. Carbon dating puts the skull to 900 years ago!

The 'The Star Child' lived to full adulthood, I'm not sure if they have determined an upper end age but we can safely assume that the child was conceived 950 to 1,000 years ago.

Chapter – 8

Let's start off by having a little look at Egypt. Cairo is based under one of the main power grid crossing areas of the world. The three main pyramids are located, sized and orientated the same as Orion's belt (the constellation). Lastly the Sphinx shows evidence of severe water damage that must have occurred prior to 6,000 years ago.

The population of the Cairo area dramatically increased around this time as the severe droughts caused all of the population to wander looking for water and they found it in the form of the Nile.

What did they find there? Who built the Sphinx? They might have also found the Pyramids already there. There is one question thought, why are the pyramids not so water damaged. As the Sphinx. When they were built the 'steps' the upper flat surfaces of the blocks, were filled in with shaped limestone blocks going from the upper block to the lower one. Basically they had a triangular shape and therefore all of the sides of the pyramid look smooth. This is a lot of effort to produce a flat surface. Why didn't they just use Limestone for all of the outer blocks and shaped the edges? That would seem to me, to be an easier option. But then again, we are looking at a construction with millions of blocks of stone.

Here is a question that I need to look into. How long would it take to plan and build a pyramid like that? Let's assume that you are 20 before you get crowned Pharaoh. Let's also assume that you might live until you are 60. Anything longer is a bonus. You don't want to die with your final resting place unfinished.

So that leaves 40 years to build something that needs 2 million stones. Let's do some basic maths. This assumes that day one you have a plan and unlimited manpower. That's 50,000 stones a year, or 137 per day. Again, assuming 365 work days a year. With 12 hours of day light that would be

11 blocks and hour or 1 block every 5 minutes. Don't forget that this is the average rate of construction.

Bearing in mind also that you need support personnel for the workers and ramp builders to allow the stones to be transported higher and higher up the pyramid. Also as you get to the higher layers, you would not be able to fit 137 blocks per day, so your initial numbers per day would have to be a lot higher.

Actually if I was building something like that I would be most worried about the ground below being able to suppose a structure weighing so much. The average weight of each stone is 2.5 tons. This goes back to my earlier estimate of between 1 and 5 tons being the most optimised for limiting shaping time and ease of transportation.

So the total weight is 2 million times 2.5 tons. That equals 5 million tons. That's an awful lot of weight to add in one place when you don't know how thick the bed rock is or where the nearest fault line is.

If 2.5 tons is the practical limit of moving carved stone efficiently then let's look at something nearly 500 times bigger.

Chapter - 9

When I came across what I am going to tell you now, I was flabbergasted. For anyone under the age of 50 that means amazed, lot and lots of times.

So my guestimate for moveable stones in between 1 and 5 tons. The average weight for the stones used in the Pyramids is 2.5 tons, which sounds quite fair. The ones used in Stonehenge vary, it depends if we are looking at the horizontal stones or the larger vertical stones, the largest of these were up to 30 tons.

Now to my mind, moving 30 tons of anything is quite a feat. I'm not sure if the galleons of the 1500's could carry that much cargo (and that would have been a collection of smaller weights creating that sort of sum total).

No, what I am going to tell you about now would probably weigh more than the entire Navy that we had back in those days. These monsters weight around 1,200 tons!

It's difficult to visualise 1,200 tons. The space shuttle (full external tanks and solid rocket boosters) weighed 2,000 tons and a Lunar ready Saturn 5 was 3,000 tons.

Actually I was slightly off earlier. Think of the big three masted sailing ships of the time of Napoleon, or think of the big Spanish galleons. These huge three masted ships could weigh up to 1,200 ton. Now picture in your mind what it would be like trying to move something of that size over land, and uphill, in the case of the Baalbek Blocks of ancient Heliopolis in Lebanon.

The first thought that popped into my mind when I saw the pictures of these massive carved rocks was why. Why would you want to create something so big that it was difficult to move? The easy answer is, to my mind, if it is not difficult for you to move.

With purely manpower, you are completely off in your estimations. I've seen theories that have ropes on each end and wheels made of solid wood around the rock. Brilliant idea and it would work for something like 5 tons but how do you lift up something like that to get it into a cradle. Secondly, wood crushes if subjected to sufficient load. I'd imagine having problems after 100 to 200 tons. As far as I am aware, the romans used nothing close to that weight of block and they were master planners and engineers. They built small and built plenty to construct whatever they planned on building.

There are several of these large (mega) stones that form the base of the temple at Baalbek. Then there are several smaller, still huge, facing stones. On top of these is the construction of the temple, using 'Roman' size stones.

If you look at the joints on these lower mega stones, it is amazing. It's such close tolerance, you just don't see that sort of tight fitting masonry normally. I'll tell you in later chapters of stone work that really blows me away, some, that seems out of this world.

Getting back to these 1,200 ton monsters, how would we move them today? The answer is, with great difficulty. From the quarry to the building site is up hill and more than a few hundred feet. No modern day transporter would be able to drive up the incline, and a crane, if it could find a level piece of ground, would only be able to swing the block from one side to the other then it would have to relocate.

So this takes us back to my question – why make something so big that it is difficult (if not impossible) to move, unless you have something that will move it.

None of the aircraft that fly today could carry one of these blocks, the biggest would struggle with more than a couple of hundred tons of freight. There was an airship being built that could carry up to 1,000 tons but this was not built because of technical problems.

What on earth (or off earth) was designed to carry these blocks?

Chapter – 10

Here is the big issue, as far as I can work out. Atlantis was not a city, it was a place.

There are two theories behind the name. One is for the people who lived on the other side of the Atlantic. The other is based on the name of the capital city Atlantis. These words are of Bolivian origin.

Let me throw around some ideas. If the people from the other side of the Atlantic (South America) were trading with the Europeans (Mesopotamians and the Egyptians) then that would explain the cocoa beans and cocaine in the Egyptian tombs.

The interesting thing here is that it's not the East coast of South America where the best evidence lies, it's the Western side.

Here, on the southern border of Bolivia you will find another one of the energy centres of the world. There are also the intriguing Nazca lines and some of the most amazing stone work in the world.

Did you know that the face of the Sphinx is that of an African Negroid face and not Egyptian? There is some information coming to light that our assumptions about Africa are completely wrong. Before the end of the last Ice Age the Africans were travelling a lot more extensively than we had ever thought that they could have. Especially to South America, where there is also a lot of evidence that they travelled and traded with the locals thousands of years ago. So where is their technology now?

Where are their boats or the evidence of them? The answer is simple, it is all buried under 430 feet of water and rotted away. They simply lost everything and reverted to simple hunter gatherers.

Chapter - 11

Why don't we assume, just for a moment, that there has never been any Alien visitations to this planet. Let us also assume that there were never any super advanced civilisations, then what would the world be like.

To answer this, we don't have to assume anything. There are places in the world where we know for a fact that no information has been passed down from either of these types of civilisations. These areas include, most of Africa, most of South America, most of North America, the old Russian state / area of Mongolia etc. The absolute best place to look is Australia.

The ancestors to the Aborigines landed in Australia 50,000 years ago. Let's look at what they achieved technologically in the years between landing and Captain Cook arriving a few hundred years ago.

I'll list everything here:-

You will notice that I haven't written anything down. That's because, as far as I am aware, they didn't invent, or create anything. 50,000 years after they landed they lived their lives like they did the first year that they were there.

Now, I'm not blaming anyone here. I'm just pointing out facts.

Let me put it another way. Why is it that most of the people in Africa a few hundred years ago lived in mud huts, but the Egyptians, only a thousand miles further north, were able to build pyramids and have the horse and chariot 5,000 years ago. The technology was there, so why didn't it spread?

There is one thing that the Aborigines are famous for, technology wise. That's the boomerang.

Having said that, boomerangs were used in Eastern and Western Australia but in the centre of the Continent they were not used, Why?. So who invented the Boomerang?

Well a boomerang was discovered in Poland that was made out of Mammoth Tusk that was 30,000 years old! So it is possible that the technology was taken to Australia.

Even more interesting, King Tutankhamen had a collection of both hunting and returning boomerangs in his tomb. He died over 3,300 years ago. So where did he get these from?

This information just gets better and better, the more we dig into it.

If we look at the other areas in the world that I mentioned earlier in this chapter, they haven't changed much either.

People visiting the deep Amazon as late as the 1950's found tribes who were living just about the same as the Aborigines.

The North American Indians did more than the Aborigines. Their clothes were more elaborate. A lot of tribes had Tip's (pronounced Tepee). These are the tall tents that we generally associate with the Indians. Not to be confused with a wigwam which is a domed shaped structure, usually made out of bent sticks and branches, whereas the tipi is made of several tall poles. But the question is, when were these invented and where?

Actually it doesn't really matter. The wigwam, or similar, is used in Mongolia which is where the American Indians originated from (that's north and south America Indians. The ones in South America just had a longer walk).

So, as far as I can see, its Tipi's and the clothes. Well, clothes wise there is not a lot of difference between what the North Americans wear to what the Mongolians, Eskimos and Siberians wear.

The people in South America don't tend to wear much, if anything. That's not too hard to work out. I'd be interested to see what the traditional clothes look like for people who live in the Cold areas of South America. Did they have to reinvent some of their clothing or are there Mongolian influences?

So, what we have established that the North American Indians did? Nothing, they just existed the same way as they always had.

So, shall we discount them then? No. There are some really strange things that have happened in North America. There is the great white serpent I'm not sure when that was created. The serpent is a structure built on the side of a hill. Then there are numerous burial chambers which is weird, because the Indians didn't bury their dead, normally. So if they didn't, who did?

It could have been the Egyptians!!!!!

The Cherokee Indian's DNA is closer to Egyptian / North African than Mongolian. Here is another interesting fact. These Cherokee Indians are more Jewish than the white Americans who call themselves Jewish!

Do you know where the Cherokees live? On the east coast. Legend says that they originated from the Great Lakes area but it is interesting that they are on the east coast. Did their ships go back to Egypt without them? Did they sink in the shallows and they settled there or were they banished? When did this occur?

Was it their ancestors that build these burial chambers like mini pyramids? Some of these chambers have been dated back to 4,000 years ago.

There have been some other amazing finds in other parts of North America. There is a 5,000 year old cemetery in Texas and one in Florida. These are on a scale unrelated to North American Indians.

There are actually lots of monuments and ancient cities in America. The North East coast has a lot of stone structure that are of undeterminable date. For so many years it was considered that only Europeans had any intelligence, but certainly in the last five years, there is a greater general acceptance that the peoples who lived there before the Europeans arrived, had far greater skills than anyone ever thought possible and our ancient history there is increasing dramatically.

That's enough about North America. Let's get to the really exciting stuff, South America.

Chapter – 12

Why is it that a lot of civilisation grew up around the Mediterranean? Was it just that there were a lot of people who lived close together who passed around information, technology and ideas around?

There are other areas around the world that had technology blips that brought them on in leaps and bounds. Countries like China and Japan had things that we, in the west, didn't. Although it is debatable how much trade there was across the centuries.

There was a grave found in China that contained the mummified remains of people buried over 2,000 years ago. The interesting thing is that they were of European origin.

So, the areas that we are going to look at next in South America are a real anomaly.

The area in question is in the Northwest corner around the country of Bolivia. It's here that we find the Nazca lines, Machu Picchu and Lake Titicaca.

A lot of people who visit Machu Picchu just go to view the site, the spectacle, but they are missing some vital information.

There are two ways to build walls where you don't use a bonding agent like cement. Dry Stone walls are built like this. With years of experience you carefully select the right stone to go in the right hole. You place them in so that they catch on each other thus holding the wall together (there is lot more to it than that). You can use shaped or unshaped stones and use cement to bond them together. It is easier if the stoned have flat sides almost brick shaped. The Romans built a lot of buildings like this. It's the same way that most churches etc were built.

There is actually a third way, and the first time I saw this I was blown away. Actually, every time I look at pictures of these walls I am amazed.

Let me go back to a comment I made earlier. Why make something difficult for yourself when you don't need to. The answer is, when it isn't difficult for you to make.

There are some walls in Machu Picchu, and other places around Bolivia, that have these walls that are almost beyond comprehension. I'm not sure how they achieved this but I can only see two ways of doing it. You either have a machine that can grind away rock very fast, or you melt the rocks. The gaps between these stones are incredibly precise.

As an aircraft engineer I have worked with metals to this sort of close tolerance and it is very time consuming. But these rocks have all of their joints like that and are a foot or more thick.

The 'how' this is done is mind blowing enough, but it's the 'why' that I really struggle with. Why spend so much time creating 100% perfection, when even 90% would be brilliant and a quarter of the time. Again it comes back to, if it's not a problem.

Let me give you a modern example. You're in Australia and you come across an Aborigine who has never seen a modern house. Through an interpreter you ask each other lots of questions.

He notices that your clothes are clean and he asks how often you wash your clothes. You would reply every week. He would ask why.

You show him your washer dryer and how you put in dirty clothes and get out dry clean ones. He'd be amazed. Washing your clothes more than once a month would seem like a waste of time if it took you hours to do it, but when you have something that you put your clothes in and walk away from returning hours later, and all of the work is done, then the work is not hard. The same goes for these bonded rocks and a lot of the other things that we come across in this book.

Chapter – 13

This is another area that really fascinates me. It's also interesting how people, mainly archaeologist, look at them.

Just in case you don't know what the Nazca lines are, they were discovered in the 1950's as aircraft started flying over the area. What they saw amazed them. From the air you see giant animal and long, long lines.

There are a couple of dozen large animals and fifty plus sets of these lines.

The good old archaeologists look at this area and tell us about the people who lived there. From that, people have speculated the how and why, people made the lines. The other area that they usually concentrate on is the animal shapes.

The best explanations are that there are religious festivals and people follow these routes. To me, this is starting at the wrong end. These animal shapes can only be seen from the air. Why would you spend time and effort creating shapes that you can't see? The white horses in England took time and effort to make, but you can see them as you approach the area on foot. These shapes on the Nazca plateau, are only seen from the air.

Before I get off track, I want to get to the important part of that area. To me, the long lines are the interesting ones.

There are basically two types of lines there. The straight, parallel rectangles that stretch for hundreds of feet, then there are the trapeziums.

How can I describe what those shapes look like? If you look on Google at Edwards Air Force base you will find the Shuttle runways in the Desert to the east. Apart from the fact they are painted and have runway numbers they look very similar.

The trapezium shapes look like a runway as you are landing on it!

Did the people who created these lines recreate the runways that they had seen, and from what they saw coming in to land?

Interesting thought.

There are also some of these line sets that seem to have a taxiway as well.

So, and here is the big question, why mark out runways in the desert so long ago? Was a runway created there by someone for their own use, and that was copied?

If some of the locals were taken aboard a flying machine and flew an approach, their perception of what a runway would look like is very different from what we see from the ground.

Something else that I have noticed is that some of the lines overlap. If we get a picture of the area and removed all of the 'newer' runways, which ones, or one, would be left?

This is what I will be doing after I publish this book and before I publish the next book containing what I have found by experimentation and what other unusual things that I have unearthed.

Runways, similar to this, have been found in various parts of the world. As the Allies jumped from island to island during the Second World War, they cleared jungles, created runways and aircraft landed. Years after the war, when people, returned to the islands, it was noticed that the locals had created runways and aircraft made from plants and trees. Why? Because they saw the Americans build runways and the great metal birds landed there. They wanted the great metal birds to return. These are called cargo cults. They have the unusual name of being called, 'Hi I'm John,' cultures because they worship the god John.

John was one of the most common names in the American forces at the time. As they interacted with the locals they would often start by introducing themselves, 'Hi I'm john.'

Chapter – 14

This is something that I really wasn't interested in until I came across a few facts that blew my socks off.

I've never really been one to grow my own crops I've never had the need, nor the desire to, so to be honest, I knew very little about the subject of farming.

There are several facts that we need to consider, and the more we look into them the more we can be astounded by how little we know. Let's start off with the basics. The crops that we grow today are very similar to the ones that were grown 5,000 years ago. Yes, in more recent years there has been some interbreeding by companies to produce crops that produce more yield and have better insect and fungus resistance. But the underlying fact is that the wheat that was eaten in ancient Greece and Egypt is the same wheat that we eat today.

Here is something that I have never considered, where does this wheat come from? The wild wheat from which ours comes from is a small plant that has very little yield. To get from that to our current crop, would take a great knowledge of plants and cross breeding, and approximately 1,000 years to create. For at least half of that time the yield would be so small that the farmer wouldn't be able to feed himself with it.

So how is it then that this crop is available as a viable crop as the world comes out of the Stone Age approximately 5,000 years ago?

Let me mention something else. Also around this time wine, beer and bread were also being made. I don't know if you have ever made beer or bread but the process can be quite complicated, especially for beer. So how do we step out of the Stone Age and have these abilities. The simple answer is, we don't.

Farming also needs several other elements. You need a fixed population to allow you time to prepare the ground and grow crops. It also requires, in the case of large cities, farmers that know how to re-energise their fields. This can be done by simply allowing a field to rest for a year and just allow grass to grow or even better to have animals graze on it, thus allowing them to re-nitrate the ground with their droppings.

Then there is the equipment and animal needs. A couple of farmers can produce enough crops to feed their families and have a little spare, but for great cities, lots of acreage is required and this will require animals, of some description, to pull the plough and to carry their produce to the markets.

As far as current time framing goes, man was basically in the Stone Age living as hunter gatherers until somewhere around 5,000 years ago. It's at this point that the first civilisations start to appear. So how then do we explain the underwater city in the Gulf of Cambay?

This city was discovered in the 1999-2000 when the national institute of ocean technology got some odd frames on their side scanning sonar. Since then, using sonar mapping, a gigantic city nine kilometres long had been mapped at a depth of twenty to forty meters. This means that the city was final swamped by the sea around 7,000 years ago as the sea levels continued to rise at the end of the last ice age.

Now here is an amazing fact, there is evidence of this city going back in to the time frame of 9,000 to 12,000 years ago, possibly even going back to 20,000 years ago.

It should be obvious to you by now that here again, we have a topic where our current paradigm just does not fit.

Chapter – 15

So let's talk about our ancestors, the great apes. This is where a lot of the anthropological theories really start to fall down.

It's a common fact that we share 99% of our DNA with Chimpanzees. That fact is actually, incorrect. In the 1970's when scientists were first able to start looking at DNA they compared some complex proteins between chimps and us, and of those, 99% were the same. When it comes to our actual DNA, it is more complicated than we would have first thought. Some parts match up perfectly, and other parts, if you move them around a bit have long strands that match up. The latest evaluations show that with this reshuffling we have a 72% commonality with chimps.

Just to put that in perspective, we have 50% DNA compatibility with squirrels!

If we assume that chimps are our closest living relatives, then we have some major issues

So, where do we come from really, we humans? What I am going to go through here is going to shock you, it may even rock your world.

Before I get to that, let's look at pre-human evolution. I have already looked at the process of us changing from small mammals at the end of the reign of the dinosaurs to the point 250,000 years ago. We have also come across Neanderthal man and Australopithecus. Well there were a few things that I missed out. Let's have a look at some of the similarities and differences.

It is known that all of the apes walk with a heel to toe walking motion. There are also plaster casts available of supposed 'Big Foot' foot prints that show the same walking motion. One of the things that I was surprised at, is that there are also plaster casts available for Neanderthal man foot prints.

The Neanderthal prints were taken from a cave that is known to have been used thousands of years ago. What is surprising is that the Big Foot foot prints and Neanderthal foot prints, look remarkably similar. They both, in fact, show this heel to toe motion.

We humans, on the other hand, walk with a heel to toe rolling motion.

All monkeys, apes and our ancestors like Australopithecus have long arms that leave their hands about mid-thigh. Our hands hang at our hips.

All monkeys and apes have a strength to body ration that is five to ten times as strong as us humans. A moderate size chimpanzee is twice as strong as any human. This strength ration is also true for Australopithecus and Neanderthal man.

In monkey Jungle in Miami Florida, there is a female monkey whose rear leg was torn off by one of the other monkeys! Now that is strength. No human could do that to another human, we simply haven't got the strength.

All of our ancestors had short necks we have long ones, they all had an inverted 'V' shaped rib cages, ours is an inverted 'U'.

It is said that there is a missing link between the ancestors that have been found, and who we are today. While this is true, and I will get to that point in a minute. The missing link, following the Darwinian process, would require a lot more changes, and therefore a lot more time, for us to change from our know ancestors to who we are now. There would have needed to be around thirty substantially different sub-species and several more millions of years.

Then there are our brains. Despite the fact that we have one of the largest brains on this planet, it's been proven time and time again that we only use around 10% of our brain.

There is a part of the brain that in a rat, if it were unfolded, would be the size of a quarter of a sheet of paper. And the rat uses all of it. In

Chimpanzees this is the size of a single sheet of paper and they use all of it. I'll come back to that in a minute. We humans have the equivalent of four sheets of paper but only use half of one sheet. Why?

In tests, using pure logic, chimpanzees beat humans every single time! They do not have speech or writing abilities that we do, but they have more powerful brains than we would have thought that they had. Using their one sheet of paper has higher logic capability than us using our half of one sheet. Yes, we have so many other functions in our brain that means that we out smart our furry cousins, but the fact is that we are somehow limited in our ability. Imagine what it would be like if we could use twice as much of our brain as we do now.

We have the ability to be able to create variable sounds. No other monkeys or apes can do that. We have virtually hairless bodies that some people have speculated that we were once creatures that lived in the sea. That might be true!

I could go on here with the differences but there is just one more item that I want to focus on.

There is the case of the missing chromosomes!

Monkeys, apes and Neanderthal man have 46. We humans have 44. So where are the missing two? As life forms grow and develop they get more chromosomes, not less.

Our history, our ancient lineage as per the fossil records only shows half of our parentage. For the other half and for some of the changes, we have to look to the stars.

Just before I give you this part of the story, if you want to verify any of these facts watch 'Everything you know is wrong' by Lloyd Pye.

According to the Sumerian tablets 400,000 years ago the Anunnaki came to this planet to extract gold. 250,000 years ago their gold extraction required mining instead of collecting from easy accessible areas. As this was going to require hard work they decided to genetically modify the existing hominoids, our ancestors. They used some of their genetic material and some genetic modifications and created us.

So, in effect we are partially genetically modified, partial earthly hominoid and partly, what we could call, Alien. When I first came across this evidence I did laugh when I thought about people who say, 'I don't believe in Aliens.' My answer will now be, 'you should do, you're partly alien.'

I was watching a video by Jim Sparks the other day and he too confirmed that Aliens had genetically modified us to create us the way that we are today.

Watch Jim's video on time travel, that again will blow your socks off.

Let's now look at how else I can back up this statement and why you have never heard of it before.

With the evidence that I have come across, and being an aircraft engineer, I'm quite happy to state that I am happy with the facts that I present in this book but let me ask you this question. If you were a scientist who worked in the field of DNA, would you want to be the one who spills to the world that we are half Alien? Where do you think that your peers would place you? I imagine that you would be finished from your current job and no-one else would want to take you on. And, this is the real kicker, you are right! But, and this is what people don't like, you are not toeing the party line. We are all supposed to believe history as we currently have it today.

I will get more deeply into more information of aliens in the next chapter but I really want to finish this one with some more facts.

As you watch the end of Lloyd's presentation he reads out details from a letter sent to him by someone who works in the field of DNA analysis but doesn't want to be identified. He suggests several major differences between our DNA and that of all other animals of the world.

Other differences between Humans and Primates.

Apes have 30 facial muscles, we have 54

An apes' arms are longer than its legs, our legs are longer than our arms.

Apes' have feet like hands, with opposable big toes for grasping. Our feet are arched and as you know, we have a big toe designed for walking and running.

Apes' have hair for insulation, females don't have any pubic hair, males don't have hair on their top lip, their nails grow quickly and they have fewer sweat glands.

Apes' eye surround (the Sclera) is brown, ours is white.

Apes and monkeys larynx and vocal cords are only capable of simple sounds.

Their ears can distinguish sounds from 1 to 8 Kilohertz, we can only hear sounds from 2 to 4 Kilohertz.

Human females have a hymen, apes don't.

Human female mammary glands are enhanced with body fat to create breasts whose sole purpose is to attract mates.

Male apes' have a penis bone called a baculum that just requires them to tense muscles for them to have an instant erection, whereas the human penis is a totally different design being essentially a sponge that gets filled with and pressurised by blood.

Ape babies are fully active from the time they are born. They can climb onto their mothers' back and hold on. A human baby wouldn't be able to do this for at least a couple of years.

I don't know about you but that list seems to establish very well that although we have some similar traits to Primates, we are a completely different species, and given the time line from Primates evolving bipedal motion, there is not enough time to make all of the changes listed above. Oh and by the way, that is not the full list of the differences between us and apes!

Thank you to whoever put that list together, I have had to make changes to fit it into my book but I collected the original information from the internet. If you know who compiled it let me know and I will reference them in the next update to this book.

We really are a poorly designed animal.

Chapter – 16

The US President, Director of the CIA and Director of National Intelligence have all been refused information on this subject. They have all known something about it. They have all known that the existence of Extra Terrestrials is true but what they haven't been given is full access disclosure.

When the Director of national intelligence phoned up the head of a Black project related to this topic, to request that he be read in, he was refused. He was told that it was information that he didn't have a need to know. When he tried to ring back, he found that his phone number had been blocked!

This is not limited to America. The former head of MI5 was shown documentary proof. Again, he knew they were out there but he just didn't know how much was known. With what he was shown his statement was 'Why wasn't I told about this, I'd have blown the lid straight away'. The response was, 'That is why they didn't tell you. You were deemed to be someone who would not hold this secret!'

This sort of conversation has happened time and time again with ultra-high ranking officials from lots of countries, including most of Europe, and a lot of other world power nations. Their Presidents and Prime Ministers alike have not been allowed access to this information.

So what it is that they have all been denied and why?

Firstly, let me answer the reason why. Let's use the head of the US Defence as an example. The reason why he wasn't read in was because in reality his title would be Head of terrestrial defence. If there was information about one of the countries of the world, then he would be told. If it was information relating to something that was happening on one of the Moon bases or on Mars, or anything relating to Aliens, then he didn't need to know.

Let's look at how it all became very secretive.

Put very simply 'The Roswell Incident' happened at the height of the cold war, the only thing that could be done was to place everything relating to UFO's and Aliens in to the Ultra Top Secret world.

Reading up on the days following the finding of the crash site, it's very interesting to read about all of the activities that were happening in the area, and all of that for a weather balloon!

When I first read the report of the incident it became immediately apparent, from several snippets, that this must have been an Alien encounter incident.

The farmer who found the crashed craft had recorded an interview with the local radio station detailing what he had seen. The day before it was due to be aired on the radio station, they were told that it would be closed down if it transmitted the interview. To prevent any problems, the farmer re-recorded the interview following the line he had been told to, reporting a downed weather balloon. As he left the building, the bewildered broadcaster followed him out of the building in shock. He asked the farmer "But what about the little green men?" The farmer replied with a smile "I didn't say they were green!"

Within a few months the farmer was seen driving a nice new pick-up truck and was known to now own a farm, which was surprising as he had previously been a tenant farmer.

He'd obviously been well paid off by the government, as being one of the few none military personnel to have actually seen the Alien bodies.

There is evidence that the Roswell space craft was shot down by a US Military beam weapon (I've only come across one reference to this).

Let's get back to these secret files and what can be done with them.

Unfortunately, having put anything related to Aliens in the secret files, it is very hard to get it brought out again, after being kept under cover and denied for so many years. No-one wants to know that their country has been lying to them for so many years, even if it was in their best interest.

There is actually one unfortunate side effect of having access to this sort of information for so long, it has been improved upon. The technology gap that they had in the 1950's is now a bigger gap in the 2010's.

There are great moves, particularly in America to get this information made public, or at least for the government to acknowledge that UFO's and Aliens do exist. Everything after that can be bought out slow time.

Some people over the years have been trying to let little secrets out of the bag.

A few years ago Ben Rich, former head of Lockheed's ultra-secret, ultra-high tech aircraft design and manufacture organisation, famously said at the end of one of his speeches 'We now have the technology to take ET home'................

As well as reading this comment from several different sources, I have also come across comments stating that this isn't true. What I do know is that the Skunk Works developed the U2 spy plane in the early 1950's and the SR-71 in the late 1950's. But what I don't know, is what they have been working on since. If the SR-71 was designed today it would take all of the world height and speed records and be the most aerodynamically advanced aircraft in the world.

So what have they been working on for the last sixty plus years?

Information that I have come across in the last few weeks has not only blown my socks off, it has sent them into orbit.

Search YouTube for Dr Steven Greer. Start off with the disclosures in 2001. I wasn't aware of these until 2015. Then watch some of the public meetings 2013 (I think) and see how former senators calmly talk about aliens from several planets (I've come across estimates of between fifty and eighty different types of Aliens!)

There are also the amazing facts that we should have all been informed about over fifty years ago. There are a couple of UFO's that some of the aliens have given to us to work on, learn from, and reverse engineer. In America alone there are at least a dozen new build UFO's.

Here are a couple more sock blowers. It's impossible to travel faster than the speed of light say the astronomers and physicists. Yup, ah, they don't bother with the speed of light it's far too slow. They use the power of thought…… Yeah, work that one out. Again, go and find some Dr Greer lectures. It's funny but he talks calmly and rationally to huge audiences about topics that just blow brain cells.

Going slightly off topic here for a minute, I've come across videos etc. on the topic of humans being on the earth for millions of years, even before the dinosaurs died out. I struggle believing that, but I would put this forward If it was possible to examine the bodies or artefacts from that time, we might find the bodies are humanoid but that doesn't mean that they are actually our human species They could be an Alien species visiting our planet a millennium ago.

These are civilisations that have had interstellar travel for eons. I look forward to seeing what they can teach us about our universe. Heck I might even get to visit the Moon in my life time!

Just in case you have come across stories of moon bases and bases on Mars, yes, at times, different species have had and utilised bases there.

So why haven't we heard more about these visitors from other worlds? Why have US President not been given access to this sort of information?

That is the subject of the next chapter.

Chapter – 17

One of the problems, in current world politics, is that people get voted into positions of ultimate power, three years later then can be dropped by the country. Is it right to give full disclosure to each and every one?

Also a lot of the information was being gained during the cold war when both sides had their fingers poised on the launch button.

During the cold war there were five occasions when nuclear missiles were nearly launched on their intended targets. Not a nice thought. So the last thing that anyone wanted was to panic launch nuclear missiles because of some alien space craft flying around. The people who needed to know were told, and that was all.

This is actually something that the Alien nations worry about the human race. In the early 1970's on a minuteman ICBM base in America a UFO was sighted hovering above the base, within a couple of minutes the missiles started going off line! This was a nuclear missile silo that was supposed to be fully protected from any electronic emissions including an IMF blast.

We were being told, these are not good for you and your planet, get rid of them.

Again why is all of this being kept secret? Who would it benefit if this information came out? Firstly, if any of these species of Aliens decided to attack the earth, then we would be powerless to stop them. Let's think about that for a minute. They have been coming to earth for thousands, if not millions of years. Any time they wanted to do us harm they could have done so. In President Eisenhower's meeting with Aliens in the early 50's (Yes, there is documentation to prove this!), they asked if they could continue monitoring and researching us, bless them.

Secondly, when could we be told about this? How about when the cold war ended? The trouble was that by then, we had so much of their technology what could the authorities tell us about without giving away the fact that the origins of the technology was not on this planet?

I have heard this a couple of times, I don't know if this is 100% fact but apparently, silicon chips and Kevlar are two Alien products that have been shared.

Apparently the story that I wrote about their being Alien technology in the SR71 Blackbird in my novel 'Adventures above the clouds' is actually correct. Not a bad guess eh.

Chapter – 18

Let's now look at some of the areas in the book that have been mentioned where there are artefacts that cannot be in the right place and time, and add to that the capabilities of any of the alien species.

If the ancient Egyptians cut and dressed the stones that were used to construct the pyramids, the Alien's capabilities were used to move them.

If we assume man's ability to do the carving and their ability to be able to lift heavy loads, this would explain most, if not all, of the anomalies that I have mentioned in this book.

Late 2014 a scientist came up with a theory that he didn't like. I know that sounds strange but he had noticed that throughout history, major events generally catastrophes, had occurred on earth about every 5 million years. He'd puzzled over what could possibly cause this. The only thing that he could come up with was a major body, something the size of a star, passing by our solar system every 5 million years. This led him to question how a star could possible do this. It turns out that the majority of stars actually occur as pairs. OK, so could our star, the Sun, be part or a pair? He didn't like the theory because no second star for our sun had ever been found, but it was the only explanation that he could think of. Then in early 2015 a star system consisting of a mid-size star and two others was observed moving away from us in a straight line. As the astronomers took their measurements they were astounded to see that this little cluster of stars passed by our solar system only 70,000 years ago. That was close enough to create some disturbances that could have created effects here on earth.

My thought on this is, although they appear to be moving directly away from us, could they in actual fact be moving in a 5 million year eccentric orbit?

So let's get back to my original point about Orion's Belt. Instead of the belt itself, could this be the direction that the planet Nuburu goes too? I came across a reference to the last time it was near earth as being 200 BC, so with a 3,600 year orbit it will put it at its furthest distance from us right now at 469 au. If you have never come across the term 'au' before, it means Astronomical unit (as opposed to Gold in Chemistry), and is the distance from the earth to the sun that is an average of 93 million miles. At that distance light from the sun takes 2.7 days to arrive (if my calculations are correct).

This is one of the basic problems that astronomers have with the Nuburu planet theory, far from the sun there is no heat from it so the planet would effectively freeze. I know that if we go underground here on earth, the temperature increases one degree in every 35 to 88 feet of depth depending, where you are in the world. Well, Nuburu is supposed to be three times the size of Earth so I assume that it would have a higher gravity and thicker atmosphere, so it is possible for it to have enough internally generated heat that it is not as affected by the cold of space and the lack of heat from the sun.

I think there are two answers here; it is possible that it or life on it doesn't exist. Or, as was covered in the previous chapter, life has existed there for many thousands of years by ways and means that we neither understand nor comprehend.

So let's look at how this paradigm shift affects our history, religion and future.

Let's look at religion first. Does the fact that we are half alien change the fact that God created us? No. He still created everything. He created half of us through natural selection here on earth and the other half on Nuburu. I don't know if Neolithic man or any of the other pre-humans were as connected to God as we are, but was it the increase in our mental and cognitive abilities that helped us believe that there was more to life than us and this life time. To be honest I don't know, it is also an area that I am not researching into.

Our history too, I feel is unaffected. The ancient Egyptians, Greeks, North American Indians, none of that history is affected in any way by the fact that we were created, and did not evolve. There are some parts of the history books that we need to change and pages and chapters to be added but most of what we have is correct.

And so to our future. Well, if we accept that within our solar system we have another race of humanoids who first visited this planet 400,000 years ago, just think of what we can learn from them. I'm sure they will want to limit what we are being told and what we can learn from them. There will no doubt be things that if we are told by them, could negatively affect us.

In fact just thinking about it, have we been drip fed technology over the centuries so that our collective intelligence has evolved. Have you noticed how much our lives have changed over the last thirty years? Electronics have given us amazing powers. Back in the 80's if I had wanted to write this book I would have had to type it. Admittedly, I could have used an electronic typewriter but all of my research would have had to be carried out in libraries and actually visiting the places that I have mentioned in this book. Although I still want to visit Bolivia, Baalbek and the Pyramids in Egypt for myself, I can view them well enough on videos on line. Also if there are any facts that I want, I can easily find them on line too. I have access to so much information that I can learn in one hour more than I could have learned in a year in the 1980's, and it costs me a lot less to do it. I am also able to complete this book on my home pc and upload it to a website that I can have it printed through that also provides world-wide distribution and advertising.

If our technology has advanced this far in the last 30 years, where will it be in another thirty years, what will we be capable of by then.

Chapter – 19

In 1902 Tesla and T. T. Brown demonstrated to the US President, on the lawn of the White House, a device that could produce electricity that didn't require coal, oil, solar, wind or nuclear energy. The device would have revolutionised the lives of everyone since then and would not have required the drilling or mining of all of the fossil fuels since then, with the ensuing pollutions. We could instead, have used these limited resources for other uses in much the same way that we use plastics and the derivatives today but still have almost unlimited reserves.

An over unity device like this, takes more energy from its surroundings that it needs to run, so it has an excess of energy, thus creating something that we can use.

I'm going to run into the limit of my comprehension in a minute, but apparently there is enough energy in each cubic centimetre of air to power the earth for a day. It's the what's, why's and how's. That I don't understand.

Using these energy devices we could have had vehicles that did not require internal combustion engines, aeroplanes that didn't require jet engines and houses that did not require manufactured electricity or coal or gas to heat and light them. Instead it was decided not to utilise this new energy as the big money people didn't want to lose out on both the fortunes and power that they were starting to amass.

That means that essentially we are still living our lives as they did in the 19th Century. Yes we have aeroplanes now that can fly across the Atlantic and Pacific, we have cars that can drive all day and cross continents and we have inside toilets and hot and cold running water, but (apart from computers) we are still back in the 1800's because we have not progressed with the technology that we have both invented ourselves, and with what we have been given.

We are therefore in the matrix, let's all take the red pill and wake up in the world that we should be living in.

What would this world look like, The future world in the new film 'Tomorrow land' would be good approximation.

It must be stated clearly that not all of the greatest inventions have come from other worlds. It's a mathematical law that if something can be achieved in one place, given the same circumstances, it can be developed somewhere else too. We are a creative lot, we humans, and we have developed our own zero point energy devices independently of the ones that we have been given.

It's similar to the fact that two people invented the television ask the same time, while living continents apart. They actually came up with two different systems. That is actually similar to the simultaneous development of the Jet engine in both England and Germany, in the 1930's

Very famously, in the early 1950's, the major American aircraft manufacturers all started development of anti-gravity aircraft. It was claimed at that time that within the decade everyone would be travelling on this new aircraft.

Within a few weeks, this was all covered up, classified above top secret, and no-one ever spoke of it again. Why? Because the people who control the world, control the power to be able to stop any sort of development like this, as I mentioned in a previous chapter.

Let me ask you this. How many people have died because we still use 200 year old technology, and how much have we destroyed of the earth's climate?

Rockets, internal combustion engines and aircraft with wings are so last century.

The next question is, what can we do about it? Dr Steven Greer does a great talk about this. Go and see if you can find it. I'll add this to the reference section at the end of the book, so that you can watch it later on. Basically, we can all help to educate the people of the world in the fact that the answer to most of the world's problems are already available. It's just that we are not being allowed to use them.

Picture every town, city and village in the world having a power supply pack that doesn't require fossil fuels and provides enough electricity so that people can see at night, cook and keep their food cold, and themselves warm at night. Imagine if these devices powered new types of aircraft, ships, lorries and cars. Within 6 months, imagine how much less pollution there would be in the air. If great power stations were needed and these were powered by this energy, then think of what you could do with it if you had unlimited energy. You would be able to leave lights on and not have to turn them off.

There is a negative side to this, this sort of energy could be used for negative uses too.

Let me change track here slightly and tell you where some of this energy is from. There is an something called zero point energy, I briefly mentioned it earlier.

There is also energy in the earth as was used in the pacific islands to stop cyclone from forming and in South Africa where hundreds of thousands of devices were used for the mining of gold millennia ago. There is a whole load of energy in the earth. Most people don't know how to tap into this, but fortunately some people do.

So how is this energy created, some of this I know and understand, and some I'm going to make an engineering guess at? When lightning strikes the earth it absorbs it. When mountains with quartz in are squeezed by earthquakes, they give off electricity, when lava flows through solid rock it creates electricity and as the earth's molten iron core rotates it too creates electricity. All of this is available to us if we can create the right sorts of devices to extract it.

One of the simplest things that can be done that only seems to have a limited following is hydrogen power. In the Caribbean, Australia, Pacific

Islands, in fact, anywhere in the tropics you can use solar energy to split water into hydrogen and oxygen. The electricity keeps the elements apart. Then you run hydrogen through a converter as the hydrogen loses its electrical charge it bonds with oxygen to form water, and gives us power. There is no need for any of these countries to currently be using fossil fuel powered vehicles.

Having read this book it's up to you. If you want to do something about helping our Extra Terrestrial friends have better relationships with us where we can benefit from their technology, and they can benefit from us then, get out there and do something good with your life.

Steven Greer was just a country ER doctor who had a dream of how he wanted to change the wrongs of the world, he was just a small cog in a big machine, but instead, he has made himself into a great one.

I know what I will be doing. I will be opening my heart and my mind up to the ET's. I'll be looking to create what used to be called UFO's (Unidentified Flying Objects), that are now called ETV's (Extra Terrestrial Vehicles) to be observed by lots of people near me.

I will be traveling around the world looking at places that have things that were impossible for ancient man to be able to make, without any help from other world influence.

I am also looking to jump on the coat tails of Brien Forrester and Steven Greer and others to help them talk to the people of the world. To help them open people's eyes to not only what they have been missing for the last one hundred years, but also to the new possibilities.

How would you like a hover car as was used in the Jetsons the Hanna Barbara cartoons of the 1970's, or stay in a moon base hotel? How would you like a two week journey around our solar system visiting all of the major plants for yourself?

With the research for this book I realise that my sci fi novels are just not sci fi enough, we could actually be there within the next ten years.

It is total feasible that I could have my 60th birthday party on the Moon, how cool would that be?

Chapter – 20

If you want to become an archaeologist, my suggestion would be to leave the ancient Egyptians, Greeks and Romans to someone else. For me, the ground breaking work would be in looking into the really ancient cultures. Who were these people, and where did the technology that they used come from? It is mind blowing to me that thousands of years before the pyramids were built (as per the current Egyptological dates) there were cities throughout the world using technology that we cannot reproduce today.

I will have to warn you though, that there will be an amount of ridicule to come from your peers, for heading down this path, but the rewards will be massive. Do you want to be someone who writes yet another paper on Egypt or on what the Romans built, or do you want to be one of the first people who accurately reports on a previously unknown culture that lived successfully 20,000 years ago.

Where is the evidence for these cultures? Some are right in front of our eyes and some are under the waves. The great pyramid of Giza has some interesting dimensions. If you take its height double it, times it by 60 then by 360 you get a distance equal to the diameter of the earth. If you take the length of one side and apply the same formula you get the circumference of the earth. That is not coincidence. That is a message from the past. It is saying 'we were here, we had great abilities.' The top of the pyramid is only half an inch off dead centre. That is such a small amount as to be insignificant. Modern buildings don't come anywhere near to as close tolerance as that.

One last interesting fact, the height of the great Pyramid is over 400 feet. It is very close to the sea level change that occurred after the last ice age. If you want to find evidence of prior civilisations then start off at that depth, the old coast line.

There is a collective knowledge gap with the human race, we seem to not remember anything from over 5,000 years ago. Just what did happen to us?

Here is the best conclusion that I can formulate. The catastrophic end of the Younger Dryas caused massive climatic changes including mega tsunamis, rising sea levels that averaged 2 inches a year for 190 years and incredible rain fall. These effects crushed our then highly intelligent ancestors 11,600 years ago. No longer were they able to fly their flying machines. They did have the ability to lift heavy rocks and carve stone intricately with ease. There might have been other things that they were capable of, but these have been lost to time and rising seas. All that we are left with are their stone remnants. There is one area that I feel needs extensive research That is the sea bed around the coasts of the world starting at a depth of 480 feet, where we are most likely to find the most evidence. We already have a few places to search including the pyramids off the Florida coast.

Chapter – 20

Just in case all you have done is read my book and haven't watched any of the videos that I have suggested. Let's assume that you really are not yet convinced that Aliens are real or that UFO's are real.

I want you to go to YouTube in a minute and watch a presentation by Charles Hall, Charlie to his friends.

Charlie was in the Air Force in the 1960's and worked as a meteorologist. His working day in in Nevada generally consisted of him releasing weather balloons in the early morning. He worked in areas 53 and 54 that were part of the Groom Lake complex that is commonly known as area 51.

Charlie's work was pretty standard apart from the tall white aliens who wandered all over the base. The Aliens had one of the areas as their living area and the other one as a working area for their Interstellar space vehicles. I know it sounds like a set up for one of my Sci Fi books, but I can assure you it is not, you need to listen to this guy talk. He is not the best public speaker but the information that he gives is enough to make your jaw hang slack.

He was there for a total of two years and has lots of conversations with the Tall Whites.

There is a great recording of Charlie being interviewed for a radio show. The presenter asks him if he had ever seen any of the Extra Terrestrial vehicles. Oh yes says Charlie, there are the short range small ones, the interstellar ones and the cargo ones. He was once picked up in one of the cargo ones when he twisted his knee and need a lift back to base.

He was given free range to roam anywhere he wanted to throughout the base. He describes the base as the Tall Whites embassy on earth, just as we have embassies in other countries.

The presenter then asks Charlie if he ever saw any of the grey liens, "No" says Charlie, "they were up in area's 55 and 56," (or something like that).

That is proof that there are at least two species of Aliens living on American soil within the borders of mainland USA.

One last one before I close. Look for the former Canadian minister of defence and see what he has to say. He has publicly stated that Alien vehicles have flown through Canadian Airspace.

I suggest that everyone reads up on this subject, the full reveal will happen sooner that we think.

The future sure is going to be interesting and exciting.

Additional items that will be worth investigating

1, Ropes of antiquity, just what are their limitations?

2, Mountains of fire. Apparently a mountain that contains a lot of quartz can become electrified by an earthquake.

3, 1012 HTZ – the frequency of gravity, that really requires more looking into.

4, The Anunnaki are these the greys and our half ancestors?

5, Nuburu, what do we know about this plant and what would life be like on a plant three times the size of ours living in space away from the sun?

6, Indian city that is now occupied that was populated from 32,000 to 9,000 years ago. What evidence is there of the early city? Who were these people? What technology did they use? As their city was covered by waters after the last ice age, where else in the world are their cities that were inhabited before 9,000 years ago and are now underwater.

7, I came across something a while ago that mentioned mass graves in what is now Texas and Florida from 5,000 years ago?

8, A meteor landed in America 10,000 years ago. Investigate.

9, Anti-gravity devices that can cause a frog to float!

Reference Material

This reference material is here to help you comprehend anything that you didn't get the first time from reading my book. It is also good to get a different person's perspective on the facts that I give you in this book. If there is something that I have written that you don't believe, just watch these YouTube clips or buy yourself other books on this subject.

1, YouTube – Lloyd Pye (his video that blew my socks off), 'Everything you know is wrong' by Lloyd Pye.

2, YouTube – Lloyd Pye 'Star child'.

3, YouTube – Steven Greer 'The Disclosure 2001'

4, YouTube – Steven Greer 'Speech 1'

5, YouTube – Steven Greer 'Citizen talks'. There are several of these, all of them interesting. The videos are a couple of hours long each but they will certainly leave you slack jawed and intrigued throughout that time.

6, Jim Sparks 'Time Travel'

Printed in Great Britain
by Amazon